WRECKING CREW

wreck·ing crew

Poems by LARRY LEVIS

University of Pittsburgh Press

Library of Congress Catalog Card Number 78–181398
ISBN 0–8229–3238–5 (cloth)
ISBN 0–8229–5226–2 (paper)
Copyright © 1972, Larry Levis
All rights reserved
Henry M. Snyder & Co., Inc., London
Manufactured in the United States of America

Acknowledgment is made to the following publications in which some of these poems first appeared: *Backwash*; *Choice*; *Crazy Horse*; *Hearse*; *Just What the Country Needs, Another Poetry Anthology*; *The Nickel Review*; *Northwest Review*; *Pebble*; *Statement*; *Syracuse Poems 1969*; *TransPacific*; and *Worksheet*.

"Train," "Los Angeles and Beyond," and "Applause" first appeared in *Down at the Santa Fe Depot*, edited by D. Kherdian and J. Baloian and published by the Giligia Press.

"Fish" and "Long Distance Runner" originally appeared in INTRO #2, edited by R. V. Cassill. Copyright © 1969 by Bantam Books, Inc. Also published in a hardcover edition by the McCall Publishing Company, 1970.

For Barbara

Contents

Wrecking Crew

The Poem You Asked For

The Poem You Asked For

My poem would eat nothing.
I tried giving it water
but it said no,

worrying me.
Day after day,
I held it up to the light,

turning it over,
but it only pressed its lips
more tightly together.

It grew sullen, like a toad
through with being teased.
I offered it all my money,

my clothes, my car with a full tank.
But the poem stared at the floor.
Finally I cupped it in

my hands, and carried it gently
out into the soft air, into the
evening traffic, wondering how

to end things between us.
For now it had begun breathing,
putting on more and

more hard rings of flesh.
And the poem demanded the food,
it drank up all the water,

beat me and took my money,
tore the faded clothes
off my back,

said Shit,
and walked slowly away,
slicking its hair down.

Said it was going
over to your place.

Magician Poems and Early Poems

Long Distance Runner

I never know how I'm doing; I just
run it, past
the stilled elm leaves.
Once I saw my
shadow in water, and

glanced back, but I was gone.
Only the ponds flashed blankly in the sunset,
stagnant with summer.
And so I run
into the mute acres of stones,

hurrying, deaf under the sky,
becoming so isolate
I could be scraped off on a fingernail—
but I slow into shouts,
into the arms that are holding me up.

The Greedy Grocer's Song
on Rueful Mountain

It's too late now for anyone
to come in.
I try to doze off
in the swept quiet of the stock room,

but I've left the door,
huge enough for a moving van,
open, and shadows of pines
fall in, darkening my hands.

I'd go on home now
if my wife hadn't run off
with the logger.
Jays scoff in the branches,

the empty road darkens,
and shadows of leaves thicken on the floor.
All the small animals,
pack rats, squirrels, shrews,
with their deep suspicions and tiny trails,

went underground a week ago.

The New Bombers

The new bombers
whistling quickly over my head tonight
are stainless as knives
that never pause for breath.

And the wings make no sound at all
as bones give
in a scuffle of dust and leaves that
falls back in ashes.

I sit tight as a locked-up engine,
among the rusting sedans,
among the unlit
neons glistening in rain like dead insect eggs.

And I hear the wind pick up bad breath
through American storm fences and old iron.

The War

He thought he could ignore the war,
and forget how
he paid for it daily—
with a silence, a sales tax.

He numbed himself to photographs
of farmers swatting flames off their faces.
He lived at least
as well as a cold rat,

waiting for his number to come up.
But he behaved himself,
already cowed
by the nightsticks that left him alone.

Wound

I've loved you
as a man loves an old wound
picked up in a razor fight

on a street nobody remembers.
Look at him:
even in the dark he touches it gently.

Magician Poems

1. The Magician's Exit Wound

All day
the sky has the look of dirty paper.
My shadow stays indoors.
I watch its step,

and plan my tricks.
This evening,
the loneliness of disappearing acts!
I think of

poking my head through the sky,
and, in those frozen pressures,
of breaking into
blood on a cloud.

2. The Magician's Ride to the Hospital

Just now
I noticed my arms,
how they act without even telling me anymore,
their preference for rain and razor blades,

or for simply dropping off,
like forgotten two-by-fours falling off
half built houses.
Now they grab at me like stubborn interns.

                I turn quickly, mirrored
in the dark glass of the ambulance,
where already
my face is wood, and painted to a doll's
astonished whites and reds.

Outside even the sky is shocked and darkens.

3. Magician's Face

One day all the smiles hardened;
pals frowned like a firing squad and closed in.
So I got lost in
cafeterias,

in the waiting rooms of airports,
and tapped my fingers,
until I was
alone as a paper scrap under someone's heel.

Then a funny thing happened.
I did a real trick—
sitting still while a plane roared off,
I made a face like

a single window smashed and bare with sky.

4. *The Magician at His Own Revival*

Once I thought my mouth was a scar
that disappeared
like spittle being wiped off of a plate.
So I shut up

and sulked
like last year's inner tube that hangs
in a noose all winter
through the rain.

I sat through the chatter.
Then somebody bared his teeth and jeered.
I rose. I called out
like a blind man drifting on the drifting ice,

for no reason at all but me, me.

5. *The Magician's Call*

Our conversation
frays like an old wire in the rain—
its thinness crackles.
And there's a silence as the phone's hung up,

as frank as someone's heels walking out.
Outside in lightning,
the palm trees whiten quickly and go bald
as the fronds crack

in the wind.
"Eat shit," says someone pushing me away;
and my father's
vanished with a smell of fear and forever

just under his breath in the static.

6. The Magician's Edge and Exit

I've got my edge now—
as a lone end of a sheet quivers on the line
and waits for the
flick of someone's nail in the wind,

and a lost
pocketknife rusts on the railings,
where the fence boards warp and blister.
Now driving I whip

the wheel back and forth—
as a frayed tire skids on the ice,
and a back fence looms like flesh turned inside out
in the noise.

And I drift through it, suddenly air.

7. The Magician Ending

After a while my lungs give
like shale keeling off without a sound.
And I don't hear anything as I let the flesh go,
and open out

like a diver,
my arms spreading beyond their own nerves,
as a shrug of stars and years
drifts through me.

Poem

I am a used-car dealer, speaking
                              a dead tongue.
I am several unclaimed hats.

I am an old Cuban in the rain,
or water pouring slowly.

I am only a naked man,
sitting up in bed,
six hours out of New York City by either
dogtrots or heartbeats
or the heavy breathing in bus depots.

Age

On the post
of an abandoned wharf
a sea gull settles,
fixes me with a hard stare,
and grows old.

The boards move gently under my feet,
we're floating.

Cool Morning Shower
in Early Spring

So.
I am becoming an elephant,
who stands listening to the rain
under great leaves
barely moving at all.

This is the way it happens.

Part Two

The Secret

I have just painted a luminous
green moth on the inside of
your thigh. We talk,
stare into the fire,
become unimportant.

I go out quietly,
shutting the door.
Wait with my big hands in my pockets.
Breathe in. Breathe out.
Watch the shadows of fish bellies twisting
over the bottom.

There's something I'm not telling.

Speeding in Utah

If it appears
as a train
you will be hearing
nothing new, but
watch as the
flatcars loaded
with moons,
sundials, menstruating
girls turning in sleep
snap by you
under a steady
light.
Under us fish
are turning, too,
on their rack of water
where they cannot
really stop
things and pause
a moment: that
is a whiskery
feel of centuries.
And even as I begin
Knowing All,
this fish turns into
a moping girl
or a cabbage gone blind
with the feel of its own leaves.

Poem

So I find myself
trailing a forefinger through the dust
on a banister,
            climbing upstairs,
where my wife
holds the instep of the moon
in her sleep.

Waking with Some Animals

Waking, I remember that
the lion is pacing the shadowy zoo.
The elephants sleep standing on all fours,
wearing huge roses fastened deep within their ears.
And things are kicked over in the darkness.

The Cycle

Tonight cows
are standing absolutely still
grass stirs under them
somewhere

as I go on tying
my shoes
quietly just before daybreak
and you are

opening your blue eyes happily
and I find myself
jumping up and down very softly
or turning somersaults

What could be simpler
than this life
we are leading gently by the halter
to waters that

are turning so clear and true
they keep vanishing altogether
leaving the grass
there and the enormous hooves silent.

Answers

Who are you?
The rumpled bed,
the silence of the forest
are here,

and I am the man who watched your knees
for months, without making a sound.

Yesterday the car
drove off without us.
The dog fell asleep a hundred times.
It began snowing again.

Your eyes fill with the morning,
with the light that is given simply,
with no questions.
Here we are.

Bus Ride

1.

Annually in grammar school
herds of butterflies
flickered slowly across the playground,
migrating I think.

I have no idea what became of them.
They have stopped it, though.

Maybe the fat man
standing quietly over there
with an ordinary, soft hat on his head
ate them all.

2.

The man boards a bus
with his heartbeats.
I get on too.
Moths drift in and out of his ears, his lips—
he is fascinating.

When his blue eyes stare into mine a moment,
they are small clocks ticking harder.

3.

I step down
gently into the street,
where a burst pipe
is leaking very clear water.

Applause

These wings buried beneath a thin cocoon
struggle quietly and open
just as people begin applauding over
by the bandstand.
      I feel like a
moth on the lip of a waterfall.

Driving East

For miles,
the snow is on all sides of me,
waiting.

I feel like
a lot of empty cattle yards,
my hinges swing open to the wind.

Poem

While the dead jay,
shotgunned and tangled on a wire,
turns over its feathers in wind,

   hands flip through newspapers in town.
And sixty
years from now my skull in the wind,
dug up by a child and jammed on a stick,
for fun.

         Dirt slips under my heels,
and I step softly out of it all,
like a girl
stepping over her fallen skirts,
or a wheel spinning off an axle,
         rushing under the moon—

as I open my eyes, blink and hold still.

Winter

I will stuff a small rag of
its sky into my pocket forever.

Wrecking Crew

Train

There is a train I'm on.
It carries scrap iron, the conductor
is hard of hearing,
and has a small dark
hole in the back of his head
that no longer troubles him.

He has a butch haircut
cropped so close I can see
underneath where the skin has died,
and is ashes.
We pass by a yard of chickens exploding,
and I try yelling to him
but when he turns
he's all smiles

and trees are slipping past, out
the window,
and small spots of oil under us
like animal droppings or the midnights
you see crossing a face,
as I see them crossing his.

Bat Angels

Sometimes they smear the evening on the air
with wings that
slap like pistons, just noticed.

In the loose fur,
their armpits fold like rags,
they leave nosebleeds on snow, and fall
like hands dropped on shoulders.
  I saw one lift straight up turning to light.

  Sometimes, out for itself,
an angel like this
comes twisting with its deadpan face
and skitters its blind jaws for meat
over the wind and weeds

It can't be caught, it's mad,
all night it wants
to chew its own blood and whimper and forget
  the flesh it drags—

while the bare rafters tick under the moon.

Mountains

It's the silence falling like ashes from the high
meadow that bothers us.

Things want to burst here—
like the slash of the roadside
glaring with shredded tires and car sickness,
broken glass and the ripped tongues of shoes.

Even the rocks are troubled
    by a deep itching inside them.

That's why the chain saws whine on like static.
That's why
men breaking for lunch in a clearing
would bite knives.

Above them
all the mountains hold their breath,
    waiting for moths to break free of their stones.

And turning back,
I stop, a dumb fist against a flower.

L.A., Loiterings

1. Convalescent Home

High on painkillers,
the old don't hear
their bones hollering
anything tonight.
                    They turn
harmless and furry, licking
themselves good-bye

They are the small animals vanishing
at the road's edge everywhere

2. The Myth

The go-go girl yawns.
The cheap dye
her mother swiped from
a five-and-ten has turned
her hair green,
but her eyes are flat
and still as thumbprints, or
the dead presidents pressed
into coins.
                    She glints
          She is like
the screen flickering in
an empty movie house
far into the night.

3. *Spider*

In the bruised doorway
that has been jimmied open,
even the dark spider shines,
tears at its belly
and moves sideways a little
on its web, swaying,

while my hand on this pencil
knows nothing,
moves back and
forth, takes hold
of things, is never sorry

Los Angeles and Beyond

1.

Off shore the ocean
is keeping its hands held under.
It turns now,

while the movie screens go on
dreaming
of bikinis yanked loose and drifting,
of upholstery slashed.

Blown to the gutter
the full-color
magazines are spreading like fish tails,
I turn all colors under the neons,
like a make-believe,
or a child who can't get his breath.

2.

I steal a car and drive softly away.
Leaves stick to the tires for a while.

For Stones

Against laws
the tongue tries to go back down the throat
it gets uncontrollable   it lies

while flickering everywhere are
knuckles, teeth, fists nobody saw, hair
drifting from wires,
eyes that stopped closing heavily and met
the ax and the train head on—
all the die-hards
who kept the faith with the stones

stones that will open at a touch, breathe
and spread like water like

plain water that is simple and against the law

Lasting

The leaves lie
still on their backs
like the skin a man swims out of
crossing an ocean.

It's late.
Insane as a child tearing up cats
on a wet afternoon,

or teeth flying at each other in a cage,

I last out the night—
            my knuckles curled, dutiful.

Airplanes

I get a gun and go
shoot an airplane full of holes,
and stare at the thing on the runway
until it's covered with rust.
This takes years.
I turn forty somewhere, waiting
for the jet underneath me to
clear its throat of burned
starlings.

Visible Gears

1.

The picture of a scared girl in panties,
taped behind a locker door,
forever.

And men punching in, men
with their mouths closed, men
who have discarded their names and
go on with it.

The iron filings are so fine
they get inhaled or drift into their eyes
as they grind the steel
that makes mouths go on closing
down, that turns
girls into dust
floating through long afternoons.

2.

When the overhead crane
got loose Clayton never knew
what hit him—
he was holding 2 coffees and a deck of cards
worn smoother, he said, than a whore.

3.

I take my last paycheck
and walk out wondering, touching
the quiet, visible gears
that aren't turning, that run
on oil and starlight and wait
patiently.

         The gears are
as still as heaven or 2 clear eyes
and the sky goes suddenly blue,
clean as a bullet hole.

Fish

For Philip Levine

The cop holds me up like a fish;
he feels the huge bones
surrounding my eyes,
and he runs a thumb under them,

lifting my eyelids
as if they were
envelopes filled with the night.
Now he turns

my head back and forth, gently,
until I'm so tame and still
I could be a tiny, plastic
skull left on the

dashboard of a junked car.
By now he's so sure of me
he chews gum,
and drops his flashlight to his side;

he could be cleaning a trout
while the pines rise into the darkness,
though tonight trout
are freezing into bits of stars

under the ice. When he lets me go
I feel numb. I feel like
a fish burned by his touch, and turn
and slip into the cold

night rippling with neons,
and the razor blades
of the poor,
and the torn mouths on posters.

Once, I thought even through this
I could go quietly as a star
turning over and over
in the deep truce of its light.

Now, I must
go on repeating the last, filthy
words on the lips
of this shrunken head,

shining out of its death in the moon—
until trout surface
with their petrified, round eyes,
and the stars begin moving.

For the Country

1.

One of them undid your blouse, then
used a pocketknife to
cut away your skirt
like he'd take
fur off some limp thing,
or slice up the belly of a fish.

Pools of rainwater shone in the sunlight,
and they took turns.

2.

After it was over,
you stared up, maybe,
at the blue sky where the shingles were missing,
the only sounds
pigeons
walking the rafters, their eyes fixed, shining,
the sound of water dripping.
The idiot drool of the cattle. Flies.

3.

You are the sweet, pregnant,
teen-age blonde thrown from the speeding car.

You are a dead, clean-shaven astronaut
orbiting perfectly forever.

You are America.
You are nobody.
I made you up.
I take pills and drive a flammable truck
until I drop.

I am the nicest guy in the world,
closing his switchblade and whistling.

4.

The plum blossoms have
been driven into a silence all
their own,
as I go on
driving an old red tractor
with a busted seat.
The teeth of its gears
chatter in the faint language
of mad farmwives who have whittled,
and sung tunelessly,
over the dog turds in their front yards,
for the last hundred years.

5.

And I will say nothing, anymore, of
my country,
nor of my wife reading about abortions,
nor of the birds that
have circled high over my
head, following me,
for days.

I will close my eyes,
and grit my teeth,
and slump down further in
my chair,
and watch what goes on
behind my eyelids:
stare at the dead horses with flowers stuck in
their mouths—

and that is the end of it.

Earl the Chicken Farmer

That summer the prices fell,
you broke the back of a stray dog
with a two-by-four.

And when your wife
was a sack full of torn wings beating
to get out,
you dragged her behind your heels
into the weeds.

Nights when girls turned in their sleep
with nothing on,
you knew even the moon listened—
as you drew blood, and
the chickens plucked each other to death.

Hunger

It goes on in
the sudden hollows of
pockets, the fat zeros
rushing out of the plates,
the space for your thumb yearning
on the police blotter.

The knife cuts into
the food before me.
The fork says nothing new.

And there is a house
broken into, abandoned,
the cold wind blowing through it,

so a snail moves out, slowly
greasing the stones,
nibbling at nothing.

And I go on eating.
I swallow it down,
I continue.

Thumb

You watch me, thumb, waiting
for orders.
When I refuse to give them,
you grow restless.

You make a dent in an ant.
You abandon a scribble
in The Great Wall of China.
You aim straight for a speck of dust.

When I die you will become a thing.
You will be slightly curved, as if
trying to point something out
to the four fingers who know the way.
We won't even have time to forgive each other.

The Town

This moon a pig spits out on a hot night.
So empty, it spins when no one
thinks of it, looks it in the face.
You can pin it down with your eye,
your little eye. Make it stop.
Let it go.

The town I grew up in
has a drug store where men
gather, since their words
fall into the tiny graves
rain makes in their tracks.
So it goes.

In the town of 20 pool cues,
of noses broken over the feel of pussy,
among the bottles of grease and candy
lining the shelves,
the men laughed,
they stole cars and left them in ditches, smoldering.
Their wives, spitting at irons, never looked up.
They grew older.

Hair slicked back in jail,
their eyes studied everything.
Big snakes pulled out of holes,
they weaned themselves, they grew quieter,
they multiplied.

When one of them died it took a day.
He did it the way
a snail curls up into its shell
and disappears. He left only a flat
spot on the earth. On a hot day.

And I drive slowly up and down the streets,
radio blaring, under
the moon's sweating thumb.

Maybe the Dead

Maybe the dead know the ant's troubles,
or the debts snails pay out with their bodies
until only the shells remain glistening,
or the sweet tooth under the worm's lip.

As a child asleep, I dreamt
the Sierras drifting out of my right side,
the Pacific coming in on my left,

until mountains became unimportant.
The sea, too, went away,

and I was beaten hard in the face with a board
in a men's room in Modesto,
and felt around, buglike, with a terrific silence—
watching a pigeon settle on a roof, and
clean itself under one wing with its beak

Untitled

It is made up of
small, dead dogs that didn't get
across the freeway,
it is made up of worn tires
and pipes bored to tears.

It is the manhandled moonlight,
it is a girl's knees suddenly weak,
it is the highway millions drive over,

and it will come out of nowhere,
like blood on a fender,
like my name called and called,

like these animal tracks I have just made
in the snow.

Unfinished Poem

Here are all the shadows that have fallen on
no one in particular
Here is the water coming in under the pier
Here is the untouchable woman who sticks out her tongue
Here is the ax handle driven into the pig's snout
Here are the separated legs of an ant, pulled off one
by one out of boredom
and the stack of dried fish left as an offering
to the bulldozer ticking in sunlight
Here is the fist of the president falling onto what he imagines
is a table full of multicolored lizards
And here is a multicolored lizard quickly fading into grass
leaving his strange tattoo in the colors of your eyes
I walk the cut road for miles
where the ground is freezing in name of the father,
and the ghost of the cracked snout, and the dull sons
wielding ax handles in the slaughterhouse Day of Our Lord
ruled by bellies. Ruled by the longings of toys
left under houses for years. Left as offerings. Dust.
Puzzles for the woman turned to a doorstep. Over which
you carried all the dead at the moment of your birth

PITT POETRY SERIES

James Den Boer, *Learning the Way*
  (1967 U.S. Award of the International Poetry Forum)
James Den Boer, *Trying To Come Apart*
Jon Anderson, *Looking for Jonathan*
Jon Anderson, *Death & Friends*
John Engels, *The Homer Mitchell Place*
Samuel Hazo, *Blood Rights*
David P. Young, *Sweating Out the Winter*
  (1968 U.S. Award of the International Poetry Forum)
Fazıl Hüsnü Dağlarca, *Selected Poems*
  (Turkish Award of the International Poetry Forum)
Jack Anderson, *The Invention of New Jersey*
Gary Gildner, *First Practice*
Gary Gildner, *Digging for Indians*
David Steingass, *Body Compass*
Shirley Kaufman, *The Floor Keeps Turning*
  (1969 U.S. Award of the International Poetry Forum)
Michael S. Harper, *Dear John, Dear Coltrane*
Ed Roberson, *When Thy King Is A Boy*
Gerald W. Barrax, *Another Kind of Rain*
Abbie Huston Evans, *Collected Poems*
Richard Shelton, *The Tattooed Desert*
  (1970 U.S. Award of the International Poetry Forum)
Adonis, *The Blood of Adonis*
  (Syria-Lebanon Award of the International Poetry Forum)
Norman Dubie, *Alehouse Sonnets*
Larry Levis, *Wrecking Crew*
  (1971 U.S. Award of the International Poetry Forum)

COLOPHON

Both type faces used in this book—the body type and the display type—were designed by Hermann Zapf, the noted German type designer. The body type is Palatino (the Linotype cutting is used here), and the display is Optima from the Stempel Type Foundry. The Palatino face, aptly named after the Italian scribe, is modern in concept but retains much of the old style detail. The Optima is something of a modern classic: a sans-serif letter with the thick and thin strokes of a classic Roman letter. By Zapf's own admission, Optima is "the best-proportioned letter I have designed."

The book was printed from the type on Warren's Olde Style Antique Wove paper by Heritage Printers, Inc. It was designed by Gary Gore.

Levis

Wrecking crew